O CHRISTMAS TREE

Louis Weber, C.E.O.
Publications International, Ltd.
7373 North Cicero Avenue
Lincolnwood, Illinois 60712

Ground Floor, 59 Gloucester Place, London W1U 8JJ

www.pilbooks.com

Manufactured in China.

8 7 6 5 4 3 2 1

ISBN 0-7853-9382-X

O CHRISTMAS TREE

Written by Sally Gilmore
Illustrated by Julie Downing

publications international, ltd.

Winter was the best time of year in Blizzard Woods. The sun was shining and the snow was perfectly crunchy underfoot. The animals played together on the icy pond.

"This is fun!" said Fawn. It was her first winter ever.

Suddenly, the animals heard a loud noise. They quickly scampered to see what it was. In a clearing, they saw some people cutting down a fir tree. When the tree toppled over, the people carried it away, laughing and singing together.

"Let's follow them," whispered Rabbit.

The animals gathered their
courage and crept up to the people's house.
When they peeked inside a window, they
saw the fir tree standing upright again. But
now it glowed with colorful lights and twinkling
decorations. The animals watched the biggest
person lift the smallest person high into the air to
place a shining star on the tippy-top of the tree.

"Ahhh," said the animals.

"Ahhh," said the people.

"It is beautiful," whispered Fawn.

"I'd like to decorate a Christmas tree, too," said Fawn, "but what would we use?"

"Well, we have berries and vines," offered Wolf.

"And nuts of all kinds," said Bear.

"There are lots of beautiful things to find in Blizzard Woods," said Rabbit.

"But first we need the perfect tree," said Fawn.

Once back in the forest, the animals were excited to share with their friends what they had seen. Wise Owl explained that it was a Christmas tree that the family of people had taken home to decorate.

"If I recall, people decorate Christmas trees to celebrate love," said Owl.

So off went the friends, into the snowy woods,
to look for a Christmas tree.

"This one is too big," said Owl.

"This one is too small," said Rabbit.

"This one is somebody's home," said Squirrel,
finding a nest.

"That one is just right," said Fawn.

And she was right. It was.

The rest of the animal friends gathered
around their Christmas tree.
They oooohed.
They ahhhhed.
They sniffed.
They snuffed.
It was agreed that the tree should
stay right there.
And they would each bring
something special with which
to decorate it.
"Be back before dark!"
said Rabbit. The animals
hurried off.

First, Bear found some acorns
stored in a hollow tree. But his
paws were too big to fit inside.
Squirrel found some pretty
holly, but it was too prickly for
his little paws.

Rabbit and Wolf spotted mistletoe high in a tree,
but no matter how they tried, they could not reach it.
And Loon found he could only carry one pinecone
at a time.

"We need to help each other!" cheered the friends.
So Squirrel gathered the nuts.
And Bear climbed high for the mistletoe.

Loon flew away with the pretty holly.

And Rabbit and Wolf had fun juggling the golden brown pinecones.

At last, the animals of Blizzard Woods were ready to decorate their Christmas tree. Their happy voices rang through the frosty forest like merry Christmas music. Paws helped paws twine vines; birds placed berries on high branches.

It had been a long time since the animals had had such fun together!

When the last pinecone was placed on the last fir bough, the animals stood back to admire their Christmas tree.

"It is lovely," said Bear.

"It is the best ever," said Rabbit.

"Something is missing," said Fawn. "Our Christmas tree needs a shining star."

The animals looked in all the shiny,
shimmery places in Blizzard Woods.
They looked at glistening icicles.

They looked at the slippery pond.

They looked at frosted leaves
and frozen spiderwebs.

But as the sky grew darker and darker, there was still no star for the tippy-top of their tree.

The animals walked back to their Christmas tree.
"Our tree is just fine," said Rabbit.
"The best ever," agreed Bear.
But Fawn stopped short. "Look!" she whispered.
"A star!"
Indeed, as night fell, a single shining star
rose high in the sky and seemed to settle at
the tippy-top of the Christmas tree.
"How is this possible?" the animals asked
one another.
"I think it is
possible because of
love," said Fawn.

O Christmas tree, O Christmas tree,
Thy leaves are so unchanging.

O Christmas tree, O Christmas tree,
Thy leaves are so unchanging.

Not only green when summer's here,
But also when 'tis cold and drear.

O Christmas tree, O Christmas tree,
Thy leaves are so unchanging.

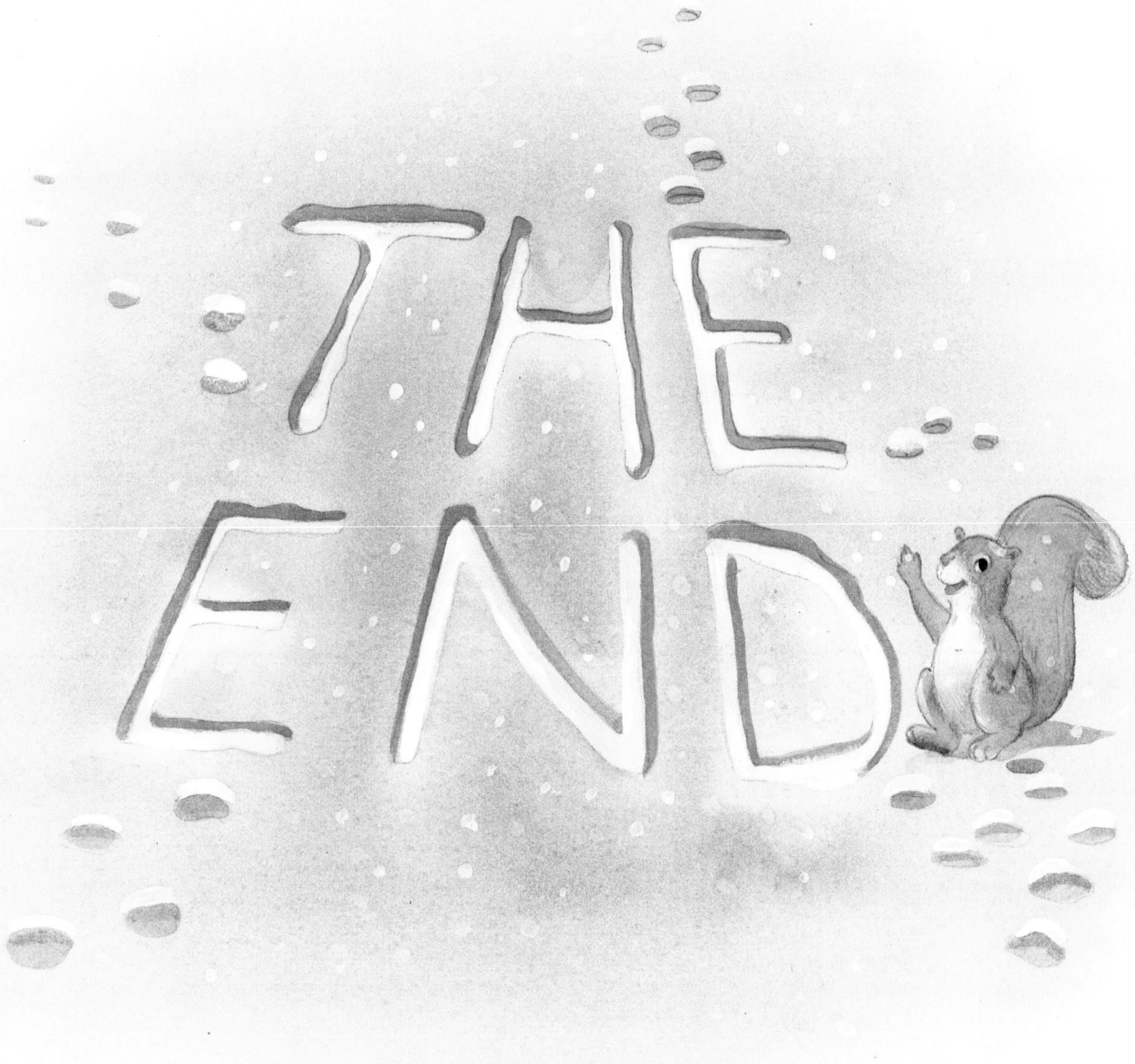
THE END